W9-BJS-267

POLICE OFFICER'S
TOOLS

ANDERS HANSON

Consulting Editor, Diane Craig, M.A./Reading Specialist

A Division of ABDO

ABDO
Publishing Company

visit us at www.abdopublishing.com

Published by ABDO Publishing Company, a division of ABDO,
P.O. Box 398166, Minneapolis, Minnesota 55439. Copyright © 2014
by Abdo Consulting Group, Inc. International copyrights reserved in all
countries. No part of this book may be reproduced in any form without
written permission from the publisher. Super SandCastle™
is a trademark and logo of ABDO Publishing Company.

Printed in the United States of America,
North Mankato, Minnesota
102013
012014

♺ PRINTED ON RECYCLED PAPER

Editor: Liz Salzmann
Content Developer: Nancy Tuminelly
Photo Credits: Shutterstock

Library of Congress Cataloging-in-Publication Data

Hanson, Anders.
  Police officer's tools / Anders Hanson.
    pages cm -- (More professional tools)
  ISBN 978-1-62403-074-1
  1. Police--Equipment and supplies--Juvenile literature. I. Title.
  HV7936.E7H36 2014
  363.2028'4--dc23
                    2013022594

Super SandCastle™ books are created by a team of professional
educators, reading specialists, and content developers around five
essential components—phonemic awareness, phonics, vocabulary,
text comprehension, and fluency—to assist young readers as they
develop reading skills and strategies and increase their general
knowledge. All books are written, reviewed, and leveled for guided
reading, early reading intervention, and Accelerated Reader®
programs for use in shared, guided, and independent reading and
writing activities to support a balanced approach to literacy
instruction.

CONTENTS

Meet a Police Officer!	3
Police Officer's Tools	4
Two-way Radios	6
Handcuffs	10
Patrol Car	14
Police Dog	18
Match Game	22
Tool Quiz	23
Glossary	24

MEET A POLICE OFFICER!

WHAT DOES A POLICE OFFICER DO?

A police officer's job is to keep people safe. When people are in danger, they call the police.

WHY DO POLICE OFFICERS NEED TOOLS?

Tools help police officers communicate, get places quickly, and find **dangerous** objects or people.

3

Two-way Radio

Handcuffs

4

Patrol Car

Police Dog

5

TWO-WAY RADIOS

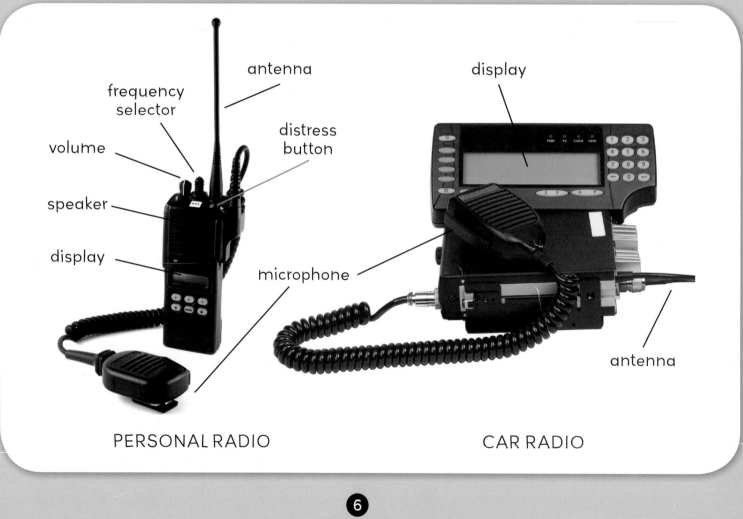

frequency selector

antenna

volume

distress button

speaker

display

display

microphone

antenna

PERSONAL RADIO

CAR RADIO

Two-way radios let officers talk to each other.

The police force works as a team. When officers can talk to each other, the team works better.

Most officers carry a personal radio with them at all times. Police cars also have radios.

7

**Officer Ally has pulled over a dangerous criminal.
She uses her two-way radio to call for backup.**

Lisa is a police **dispatcher.**
She directs the officers over the radio.

HANDCUFFS

chain

lock

rotating arm

Police officers use handcuffs to restrain suspects.

Handcuffs go around a **suspect's** wrists. They lock tightly.

Handcuffs prevent suspects from using their hands. That makes it hard for them to hurt anyone or escape.

Officer George handcuffs the suspect's hands behind her back. Handcuffs work best when they are behind the body.

Officer Brady arrests a suspect.
He will be safer after the handcuffs are on.

PATROL CAR

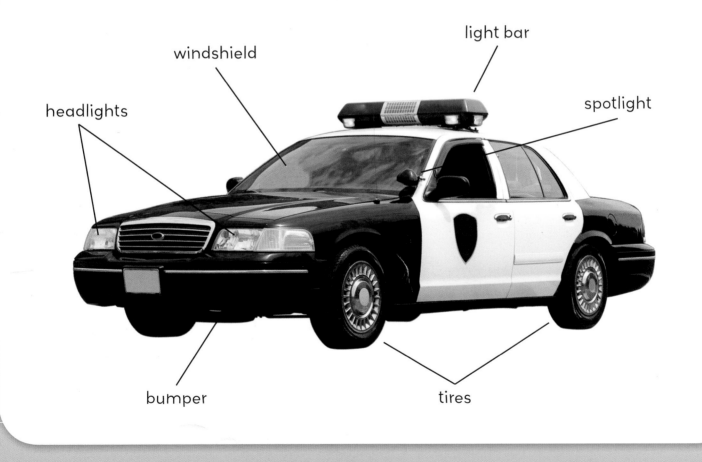

headlights

windshield

light bar

spotlight

bumper

tires

Patrol cars help officers get places quickly.

Police also use patrol cars to chase criminals, move **suspects**, and patrol neighborhoods.

Most patrol cars have flashing lights, **sirens**, radios, computers, and video cameras.

Officer Dan sees an abandoned car. He uses the computer to find the owner. He types in the license plate number.

Officer Tony arrests a suspect. He will drive the suspect to the police station. The suspect will sit in the back seat.

POLICE DOG

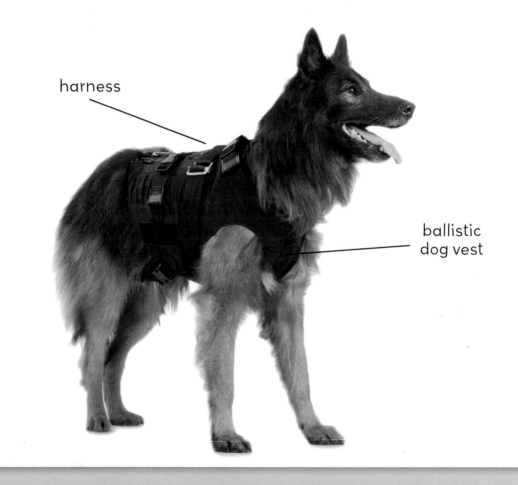

harness

ballistic dog vest

Police dogs help officers track and arrest criminals.

Police dogs help in other ways too. They can find **bombs**, weapons, people, and illegal drugs.

Most police forces have special **units** with police dogs. They are called K-9 units.

Police dogs are chosen and trained carefully. Only the healthiest and smartest dogs become police dogs.

**Dogs can smell much better than people.
Roscoe has been trained to sniff out drugs.**

MATCH THE WORDS TO THE PICTURES!

The answers are on the bottom of the page.

MATCH GAME

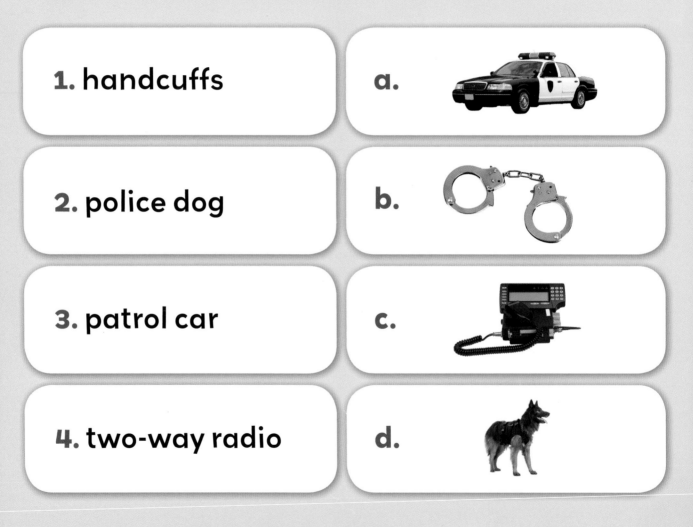

1. handcuffs

a.

2. police dog

b.

3. patrol car

c.

4. two-way radio

d.

TEST YOUR TOOL KNOWLEDGE!

The answers are on the bottom of the page.

1.

The police force works as a team.

TRUE OR FALSE?

2.

Handcuffs go around a **suspect's** elbows.

TRUE OR FALSE?

3.

Patrol cars never have computers.

TRUE OR FALSE?

4.

Police dogs are trained carefully.

TRUE OR FALSE?

TOOL QUIZ

Answers: 1) true 2) false 3) false 4) true

GLOSSARY

badge – a small sign or symbol worn to show someone's job or rank.

bomb – a container filled with explosives that is used to destroy people or things.

dangerous – able or likely to cause harm or injury.

dispatcher – a person who makes sure people go to the right places and relays messages between them.

license plate – a flat piece of metal with letters and numbers on it that is attached to a car. Every car has its own license plate number.

portable – easily moved or carried.

restrain – to keep someone under control.

siren – a device that makes a loud sound as a signal or warning.

suspect – a person who is thought to have committed a crime.

unit – a person or group that is part of a larger group with a common goal or purpose.